250 *New* Continuous-Line Quilting Designs

Laura Lee Fritz

C&T PUBLISHING

Text and Artwork copyright © 2011 by Laura Lee Fritz

Photography copyright © 2011 by C&T Publishing, Inc.

Publisher: Amy Marson

Creative Director: Gailen Runge

Acquisitions Editor: Susanne Woods

Editor: Gailen Runge

Cover/Book Designer: Kristy Zacharias

Production Coordinator: Jessica Jenkins

Production Editor: Julia Cianci

Illustrator: Laura Lee Fritz

Photography by Christina Carty-Francis and Diane Pedersen of C&T Publishing, Inc., unless otherwise noted

Published by C&T Publishing, Inc., P.O. Box 1456, Lafayette, CA 94549

Library of Congress Cataloging-in-Publication Data

Fritz, Laura Lee.

 250 new continuous-line quilting designs : for hand, machine & longarm quilters / Laura Lee Fritz.

   p. cm.

 ISBN 978-1-60705-505-1 (soft cover)

1. a Quilting--Patterns. 2. a Quilts--Design. I. Title. II. Title: Two hundred fifty new continuous-line quilting designs.

 TT835.F75725 2011

 746.46--dc22

                              2011004023

 Printed in China

 10 9 8 7 6 5 4 3 2 1

Heroic Moments

The Wilderness File

Globe Trotting

Oldtime Cowboys

Got An Angle?
Scrolls and Angles

What You Can Do with These Designs

You can add beauty and special meaning to your quilting projects by using the graceful continuous-line images shown in the following pages. Whether you are quilting by hand, home sewing machine, or with a long-arm machine, this collection of designs will be a generous resource library.

How I use this book

I have one copy of the book for quick thumb through, and another working copy that I have the spine cut off. The local copy shop charged me $1 to cut off the spine. Each page then goes into a sheet protector, in a 3-ring binder. As I use a drawing from a page, that page goes into my printer/copier with enlarging features, I make one copy the original size. Then I cut it up into the individual images, and enlarge the ones I need for the project. The enlargements and the cut up pieces go into a new sheet protector just behind the original page in the binder, for use again. Some of my designs have half a dozen different sizes in that set.

Transferring the Designs

If you aren't ready to make the leap into free-motion quilting, there are simple steps to follow to transfer the designs onto your quilt top.

1. You can trace your designs onto water-soluble stabilizer with a permanent pen (Sharpie and Pilot are good choices) and quilt through it as the topmost layer of your quilt. Try the Solvy stabilizers made by Sulky, or Dissolve from Superior Threads, as they really do wash out of the cloth.

Dissolve and Solvy are the same material, different suppliers. Sulky also makes FabriSolvy, which can be drawn upon with pencil, but will not rip away from the stitching line. It will wash away. Sulky makes a Printable Solvy, which can be printed on a home computer printer/copier. Dissolve/Solvy

can be used to accurately draw and quilt images onto quilts, and to lubricate tender threads for use on difficult fabrics. Draw on Dissolve's smooth side with a Sharpie pen—black only! Because of the nature of the medium, the pen line will not bleed through onto the source material. The complete transparency of Dissolve makes it easy to place the film over a quilt area, choosing to keep stitching lines from riding over seam junctions. If the project is a whole-cloth quilt larger than the 47" width, two pieces can be joined by ironing (use a press cloth) the bumpy sides to each other. In that case you will draw on the smooth side of one piece, and the bumpy side of the other, but you will hardly notice the difference if you are using the wider fine-point pen; only the ultra-fine-point pen will stumble on the miniscule bumps.

The toughness of Dissolve/Solvy makes it easy to pin securely to the quilt. Pin well enough that your stitching in all directions will not cause the film to travel with the sewing line. Sew directly over your drawn line, except where you want to intentionally revise the image to fit your block, or make a corrective revision where you may have veered away from your intended path. An example of that circumstance would be if you veered from a line coming up the leg of a bird image; you'd be able to intentionally veer off the other side of the leg to keep it from being too skinny or too wide.

To remove the Dissolve from an isolated quilting of an image, simply rip it away from the quilt. Some of it will remain in small details. You can pick at it with the large eye of an embroidery needle or your fingernails in areas where you don't want to add water. Otherwise, spritz it with a spray of water or dab a water drop with your fingertip to dissolve the remnants.

Sew directly on your pattern lines. Pull away the largest chunks of the plastic-like material, then mop up the remaining fragments with a wet piece of cloth or a damp scrap of cotton/poly blend batting. I prefer using the batting to mop up because it holds water, scrubs without roughing up your quilt top, and doesn't leave shreds of itself behind.

A warning: If you leave larger pieces of the Solvy or Dissolve on the quilt after dampening, they will turn to slime and dry on the quilt; the quilt will need a thorough washing.

To remove a sheet of Dissolve used to quilt a whole-cloth design, it is easier to toss the whole project into a wash basin or washing machine and launder it off. Simply spraying a large area with water is going to melt it into the fabric like a plastic coating rather than remove it, so remember, rip and spritz, or wash it away. Another use for Dissolve is to lubricate your stitching line over difficult fabrics. Some threads are too tender to quilt onto high thread-count cottons, such as some batiks. Other fabrics that torture thread include: the white-on-whites (and white on colors) that have a generous application of the white print (which is really a layer of paint); fusible appliqués; glitters applied to fabric with a glue surface; photo transfers (the stiff ones); and decorator prints that have heavy stain-proof coatings. These surfaces, and the cheap finishes from dollar-a-yard fabrics, act as a knife edge against the threads. By pinning on a layer of Dissolve over these trouble spots, those tender threads can be used without breaking.

2. Another option is to draw directly onto your quilt top with a washable marker. You will need a light source for this method.

A recycled sliding-window pane (still framed) or glass door panel from a shower enclosure will serve you well as a light table.

Lay this glass panel over a quilt frame or sawhorse set, place a light source such as a four foot fluorescent shop light below the "table." Now spread your quilt top on top of the glass and turn the light on.

Slide your drawings under the quilt, and position as desired.

It becomes evident that clean white paper and bold black drawing lines will project best through the cloth.

In time this tracing will train your eye and hand, and you can draw your own patterns to increase your collection.

Sizing Your Designs

The primary quilt design for a block should fill about two-thirds of the block. If the background is closely quilted, a recessed dimension will make the primary design stand out more clearly. A loosely quilted background with a highly detailed primary image will have the opposite effect; the background will puff up around the detailed image.

Negative Space

Unquilted areas of a quilt are referred to as negative space. Between your leaves and textures, for example, the blank shapes can be large or small, clumsy shapes or graceful. Be observant of them. A poorly balanced design will have a negative space that is confused with the image; a negative space can be so large that the quilt seems to be underquilted, or so small that the quilting lines are hard to interpret.

Hints for Repeated Images

A row of leaves in varying directions looks more natural

When you repeat designs to create a row or border, connect the designs with part of your supporting or backdrop design.

If you are planning a leafy border, avoid using a "row" of leaves. Create a more natural look by tilting each leaf in a different direction. Varying the size—or shape—of the leaves will help them fit within the space of the border, and will make the design less static.

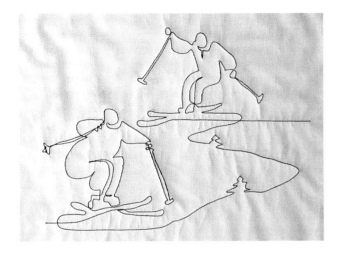

Transitional Quilting Lines

When you are planning the background design for the borders, consider "crossing the lines" into the quilt block area. This creates a smooth transition between the two areas, and you can work all your side borders as you progress down the quilt.

Keep transition and escape routes in mind; they need to be consistent with the shape or feel of the background quilting in order to remain invisible.

Using Border Designs

Once you choose a border design, you have three decisions to make: what direction to face the design; how to space or fit the border pattern to the length of the fabric border; and what to do in the corners.

1. Are all borders to be viewed in the same direction? A wall quilt would be so viewed, in which case the borders all have the top of the design facing the same way (you would have to customize the borders considerably to make them run vertically, but it gets done all the time). Or is it a throw quilt and the borders could all face outward or inward? A bed quilt may look great with a border across the pillows, with the top to the head of the bed; the lower border would also have its top to the head, and side borders top to the middle, so when viewed from the sides they are right side up.

2. Fit the border images within the span of the border. If the length of fabric causes you to end mid-image, then choose a "tight" spot between two images to extend a simple line an extra ¼"–¾" to spread the border. Repeat the spread each time you come to the same repeat in the border. This means doing a little math: If you need 4" more on a border design that is repeated nine times, then add ½" between each repeat eight times. In the same manner, you can shrink space between images, and repeat the shrinkage each time you come to a repeat of the place you compacted the design. The spread or compaction may be different for the side borders than for the top/bottom borders, as the border length will be different.

An alternative to spreading or shrinking is to divide the border design in half, with half of it facing the other in a mirror image. If you choose this route, add an extra design between them in the middle of the border span. An example of this is the Bridge Motif that is already drawn that way.

Spacing borders as an overall repeat of the row means you also need to see how much space remains, if any, after you determine the number of repeats. If you can fit nine repeats of a border design with 4" left over, you would spread each row apart by a half inch. Here is the formula for figuring the amount to spread the designs: Take the number of inches you need to fill (what is "left over" after all the full repeats), and divide it by how many "spaces" between the repeats. So 6" divided by nine "spaces" (ten rows of design) would mean I need to space the rows apart by ⅔", or, for ease of measuring, just less than ¾".

3. Corner designs may be added to provide a transition between the horizontal and vertical borders. Ideally one of the images in the border will fit the corner block. You may draw a simple curved connecting line between each of the two borders, sometimes getting a bit creative when choosing where to connect the lines. You may choose a feature image or a background image, or possibly draw a new version of some idea in the border. Another possibility is to launch a new idea for a corner, such as a sunburst that joins the borders of birds at work in the surf.

Customizing Your Projects

To achieve a refined look to your quilting, follow these designs with a stylus laser light (if you are working on a long-arm machine), or by stitching over a tracing you've drawn with a black Sharpie pen on Dissolve (or Solvy). Add any improvements to the design that might make you like it better.

Tip

Some lines are drawn "apart" to show you the stitching path, but you may get a lovelier pattern if you sew the lines closer together. When I draw the haunches of a horse, I like the big leg muscle to be outlined, but if I quilt a distinct space between the line going up around the muscle and the same outline returning to the horse's belly, it doesn't look as realistic as if I sew the entry and exit lines close enough to read as one outline.

Funky Chickens

For a whimsical or a folk-art look, draw or quilt freehand, following the design that you have right in front of you. Looking at my first book in this series, you can tell where the editors sometimes chose my looser freehand quilting renditions rather than my drawings.

Create your own whole-block motifs by enlarging an image (or set of images) to fill the block to within an inch of the seams. All the areas within the block that are not filled with the image need to be completed. Could a secondary image be added to fill the blanks? Or an opposing-direction texture be used as fill? What about adding an extension or flourish to the design to complete the block? The goal is to not leave any area unquilted that would loft above the feature design, competing for center stage. Connect all the design areas you add to the main image(s). Examples include Garden-Pine Tree, Canyon Canoer, Duck Breakfast, Polar Bear, Alaska Adventure Plane, Burro in the Desert Block, Legendary Longhorn Steer block, and others.

To join various designs to make your own borders, find the idea that connects the images: Flowers may connect insects together, leaves connect flowers, a landscape connects horses, or prairie grasses connect pheasants. Be sure to make your drawings of the connecting imagery large enough to fill the negative spaces.

A design can be "entered" from many choices of location: Any foot of a horse provides two entry points; its tail provides another entry point. To start a horse image near the face or along its back would be distracting. Try some options and choose the least noticeable one.

For machine quilting, how do you get a perfect stitch length? Just pay attention as you work, and practice before doing an intricate design.

Sometimes you will need to slow your needle speed for the shorter-line designs (an insect) and speed it up again for the long smooth shapes (a calla lily next to the insect). Practice will show you where you need to pay more attention, and where you need to change your speed to control stitch and shape quality.

Start Quilting

You just need to practice machine quilting in order to find your rhythm, and learn to sew at a constant speed.

WARMUP Tip

Begin by tracing the designs with your fingertips or a pencil to practice the paths, and you will learn to stitch many of them free-hand. This tracing makes the pattern a physical memory and helps you quilt more smoothly.

HOW TO BEGIN SEWING A Continuous-Line QUILTING DESIGN

Note any pattern sections where you change sewing direction, sew over an area twice, or sew over an existing line of stitching. You may find it helpful to draw arrows using a highlighter marker on the pattern to guide you.

For most of the patterns the starting and stopping points are clear. You can start at either end of the pattern and sew left to right or right to left.

In most cases, to repeat a pattern, the second pattern starts where the one before left off. You may want to sketch the continuation of the pattern so it is clear to your mind's eye which direction you will sew to continue the pattern.

When you start or end a line of quilting, or when your top thread or bobbin is depleted, knot the end(s) of your stitching line and thread a needle with the thread tails. Use a long-eye sharp embroidery needle for the tail so both threads will fit through at once. Try wrapping the pair of threads around the eye tightly, pinch the thread to hold the tiny loops as you withdraw the needle, then slip the eye over these tight little loops. Sew these ends by sliding the needle back along your quilting line, pull the needle out, bury the knot into the batting, and cut the tail.

A Word About Art

Throughout history quilts have represented people's lives, often expressing a love of story as well as love of color. Many of us don't sit down to conjure up "pretty pictures," so we say, "I'm not an artist."

Being an artist is all in the practice of art. Those of us who make pretty lines attract people who value pretty lines. If we create bold, abstract lines we attract those who value that form. Folk art is a more spontaneous art form; we just need to make the story unfold. There are vast numbers of people who are attracted to folk art for its direct simplicity.

It is sufficient to practice your craft in an expressive way, and follow the path of just "doing it." You will begin to see the world with a greater attention to what it truly looks and feels like, and those observations will appear in your work. Now you are an artist.

PLEASE NOTE

All designs featured in the black and white photographs can also be traced and used in your quilts.

Edge of Town

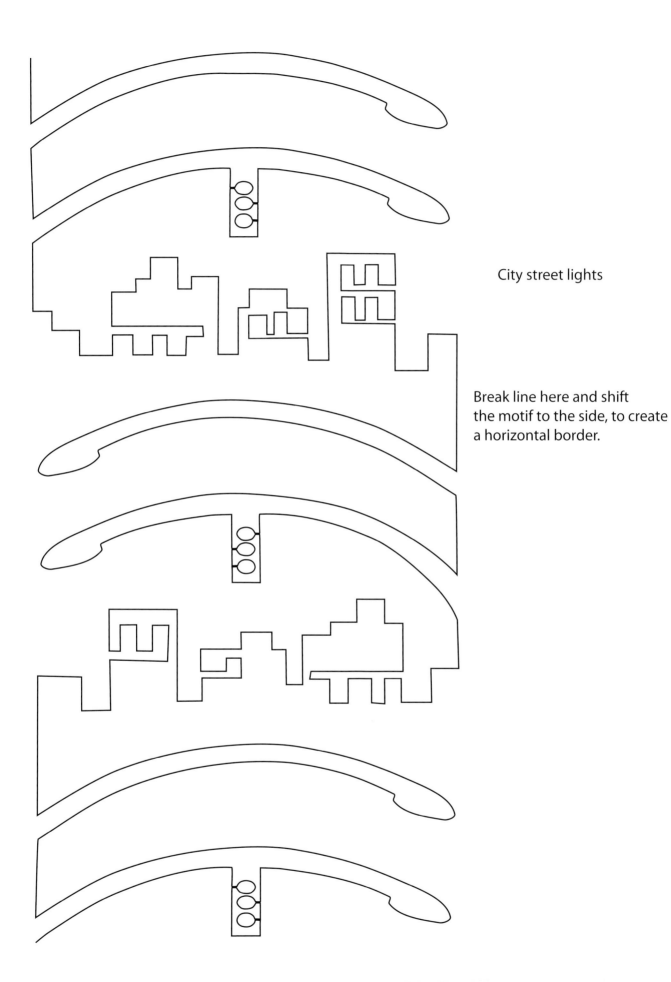

City street lights

Break line here and shift
the motif to the side, to create
a horizontal border.

City park

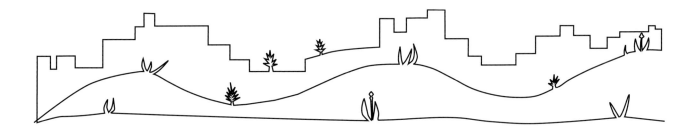

City park repeating for longer border

City street arrows border

Highway lights border

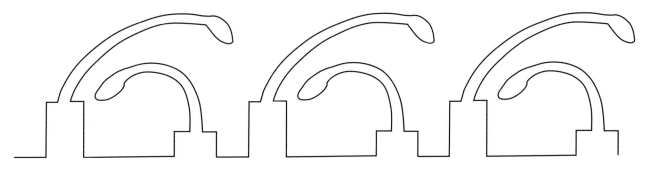

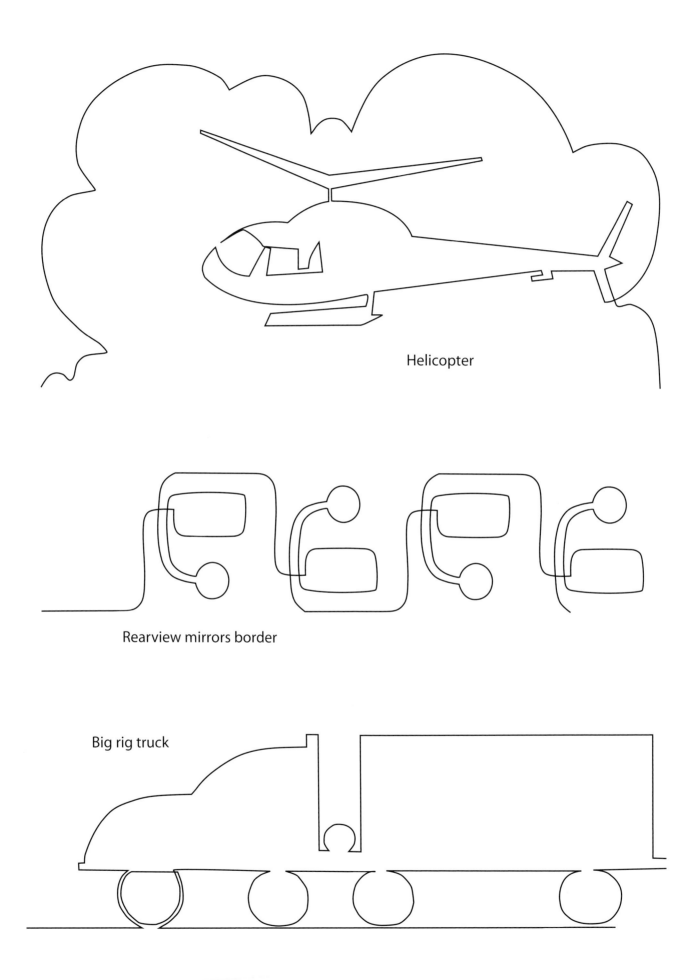

Helicopter

Rearview mirrors border

Big rig truck

Hot air balloon

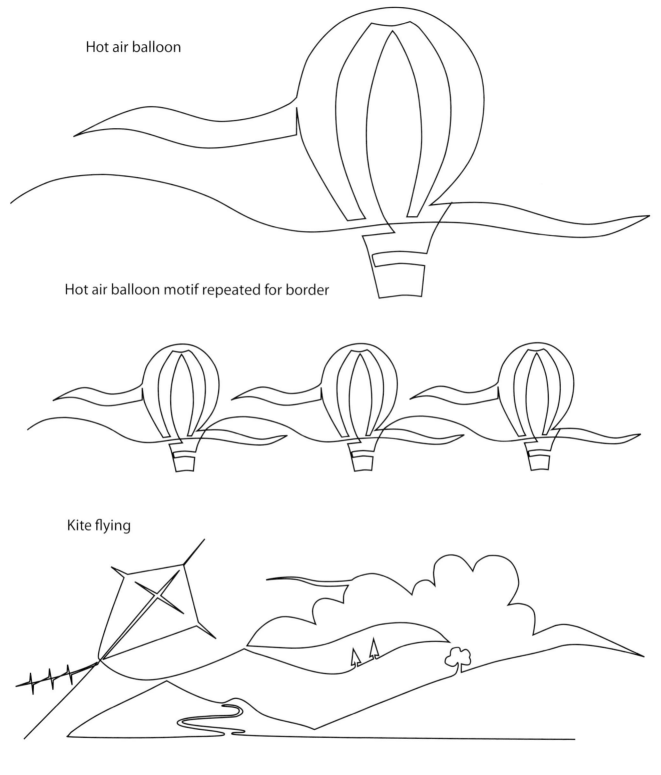

Hot air balloon motif repeated for border

Kite flying

Kite flying motif repeated for border design

Wild rose block

Garden with pine tree

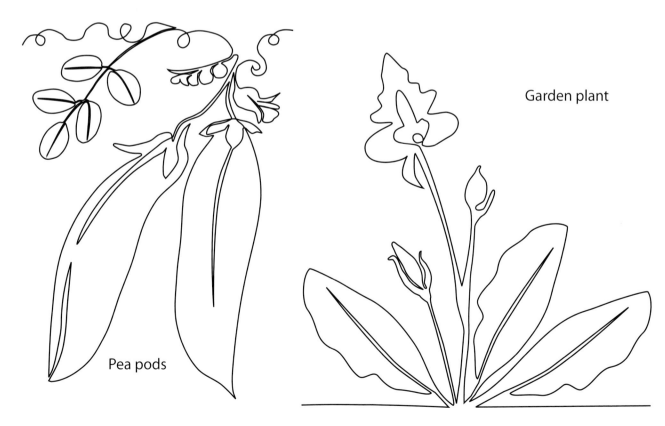

Garden plant

Pea pods

Prairie dog

Field mouse

Chicks in chat

Young hen

Young rooster

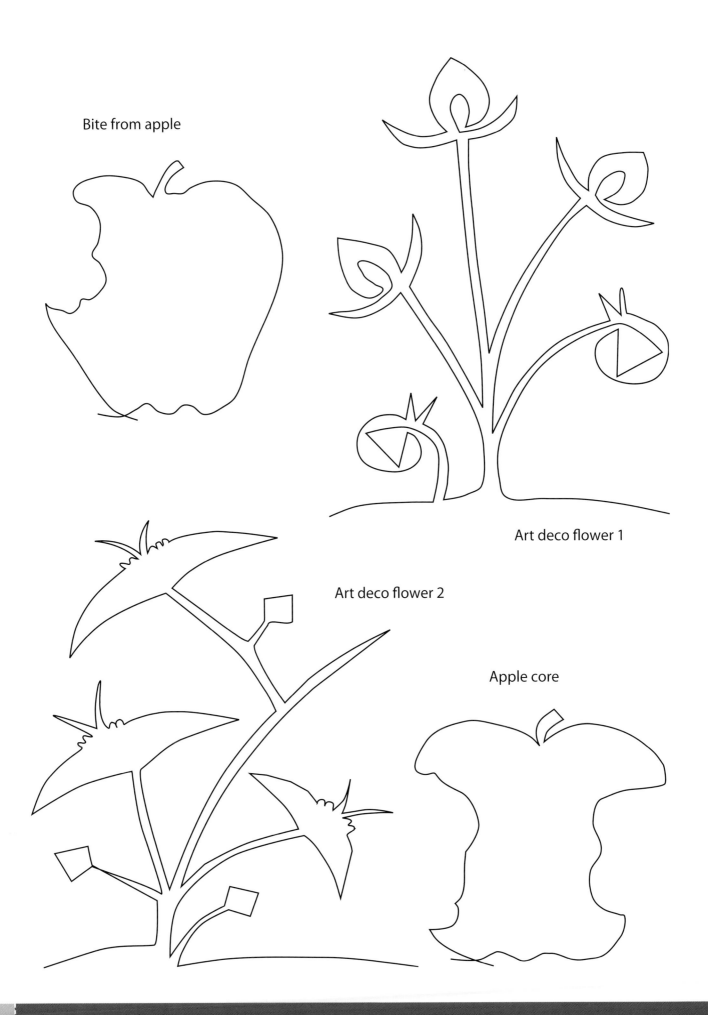

Bite from apple

Art deco flower 1

Art deco flower 2

Apple core

Mouse Everywhere: repeatable border, reversed for alternate rows

These mice make a great looking border even if you shorten the rows' height to make short long mouses, see the same mouse on the other mouse page

A mouse and her cheese

Five Bunnies

Cats on the fence

Cows in a row

Dogs swimming

Cartoon-like little kids trucks border

Minkee animal shapes

These are extra easy, and great to do in reverse-appliqued Minkee: stack three layers of Minkee, two right-side up, one right side down for the backing. Draw these shapes onto Solvy, pin to Minkee top layer (it will be your "background color"). Sew the shapes through all layers. Cut away background area of top Minkee layer, leaving ⅛″ raw edge allowance. Stitch the three raw outer edges together, leave hem raw.

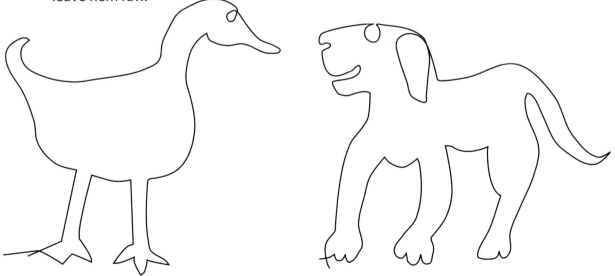

Baseball

Baseball

Pitcher's ready

The pitch

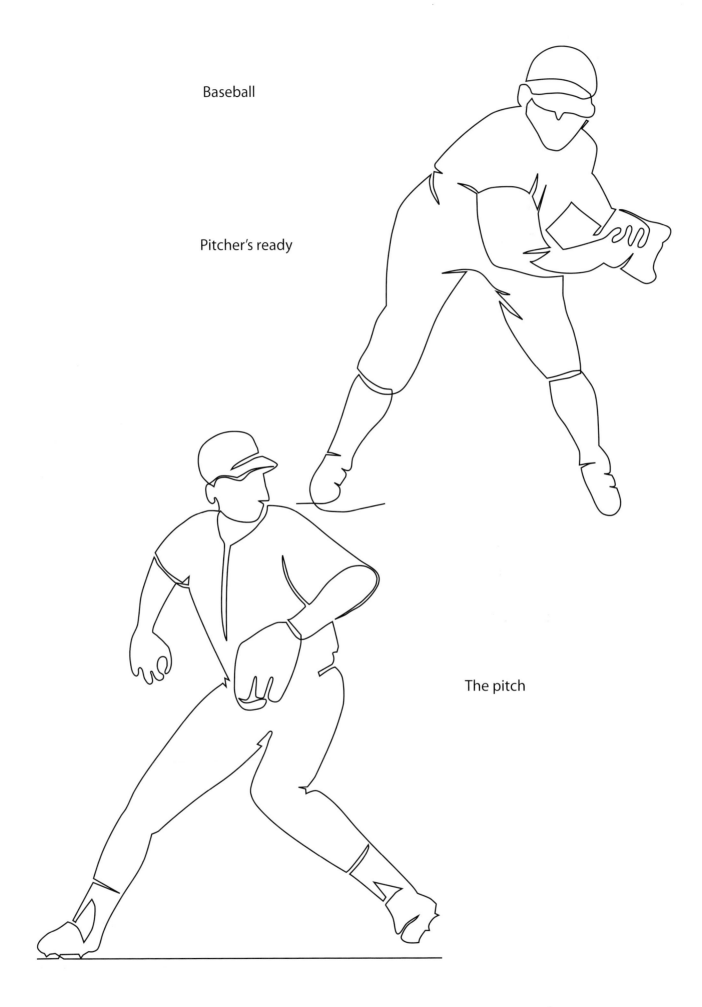

Baseball

And the pitch is sent

The wind-up

Baseball Catcher

Baseball Southpaw

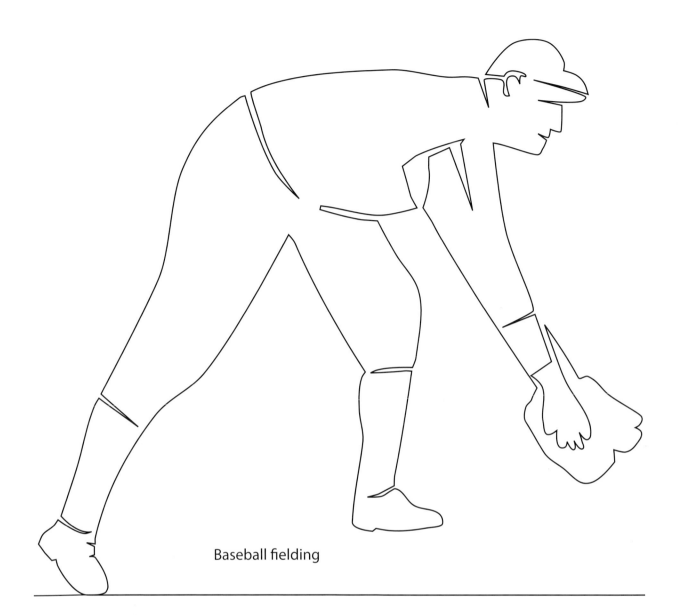

Baseball fielding

Baseball slide

Wetlands

Duck pond
three views

Rather than repeating one scene
throughout a quilt, I like to repeat
a selection of variations.

Not only is this more interesting,
it is more natural.

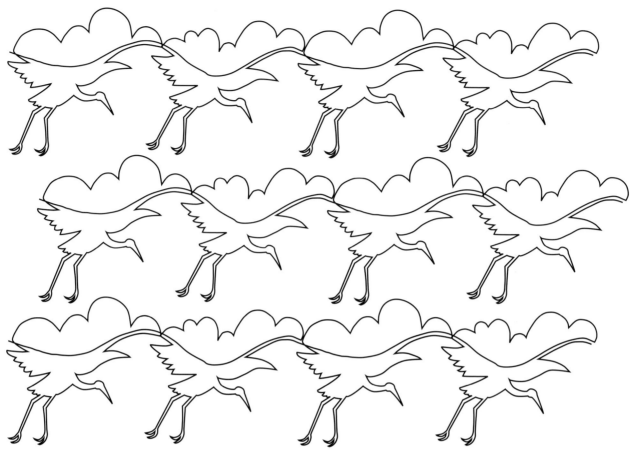

Crane and cloud border

offset for repeating as
an overall quilting design.

Crane fishing

Crane and duck motif

Duck breakfast

As lovely as any of these images would be alone, they are
more beautiful in the context of a story about their lives.

Crane with frog

Preening duck

Frogs at the
pond surface

Pond turtle

River otter

Seagull walking

Pelican with
his dinner

The pelican, with his action-packed posture, is without a doubt the leading man of any scene you will quilt him into.

The seagull is his supporting actor, while the gull has character, his job is setting the scene from the sidelines.

Flamingo pair

Outer space
rocket

Alligator

Heroic Moments

Rodeo bull rider 1

Birds on the wire

Bucking bronco at the rodeo

Montana butte country

Bull rider being tossed

Bison and baby

Mount Rushmore

Mountain goats

Barn swallow

Alaska adventure plane

The Wilderness File

Tree stand

Whitetail deer

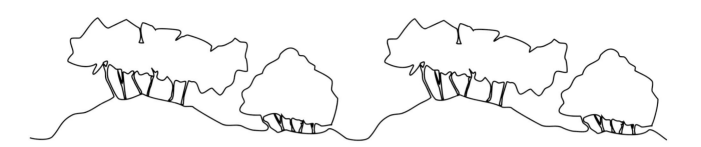

Tree stands on the knolls

Young
Whitetail
deer

Log cabin

Caribou

Wolf dog

Elk bull

Black bear

Raven

Polar bear

Globe Trotting

Cashmere goats at the pyramids

Giraffe running

Elephant 1

Elephant 2

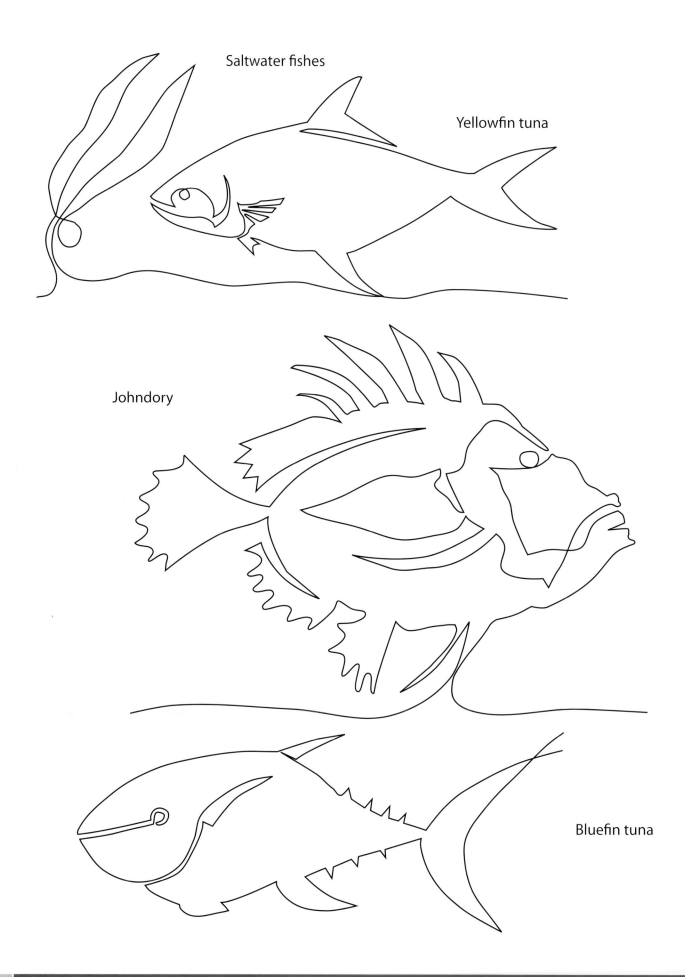

Saltwater fishes

Yellowfin tuna

Johndory

Bluefin tuna

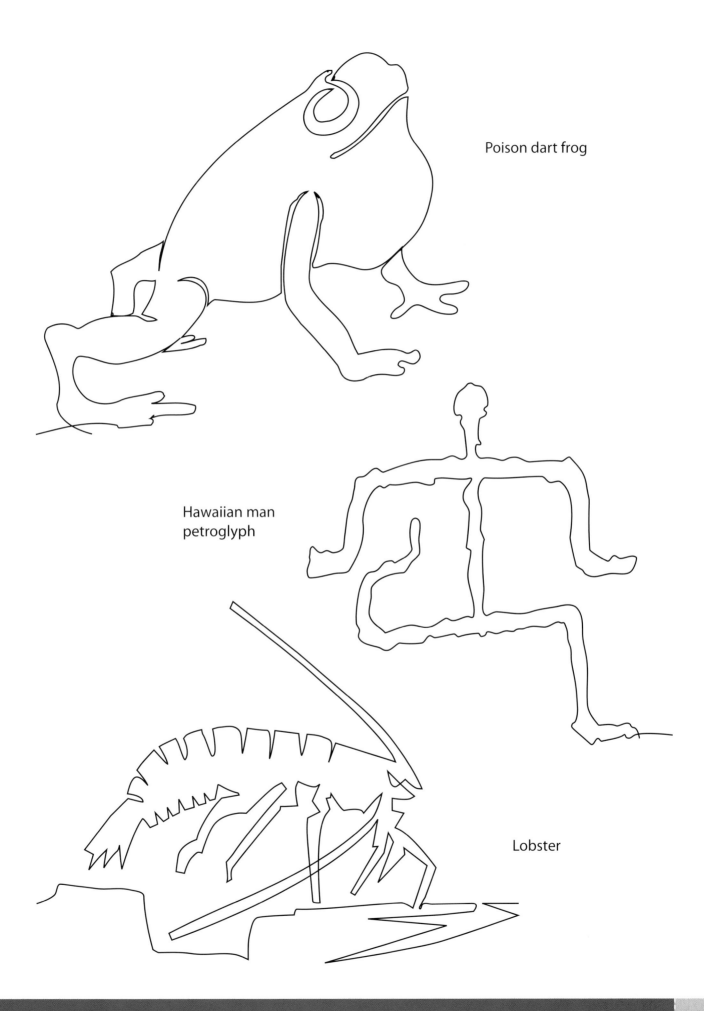

Poison dart frog

Hawaiian man
petroglyph

Lobster

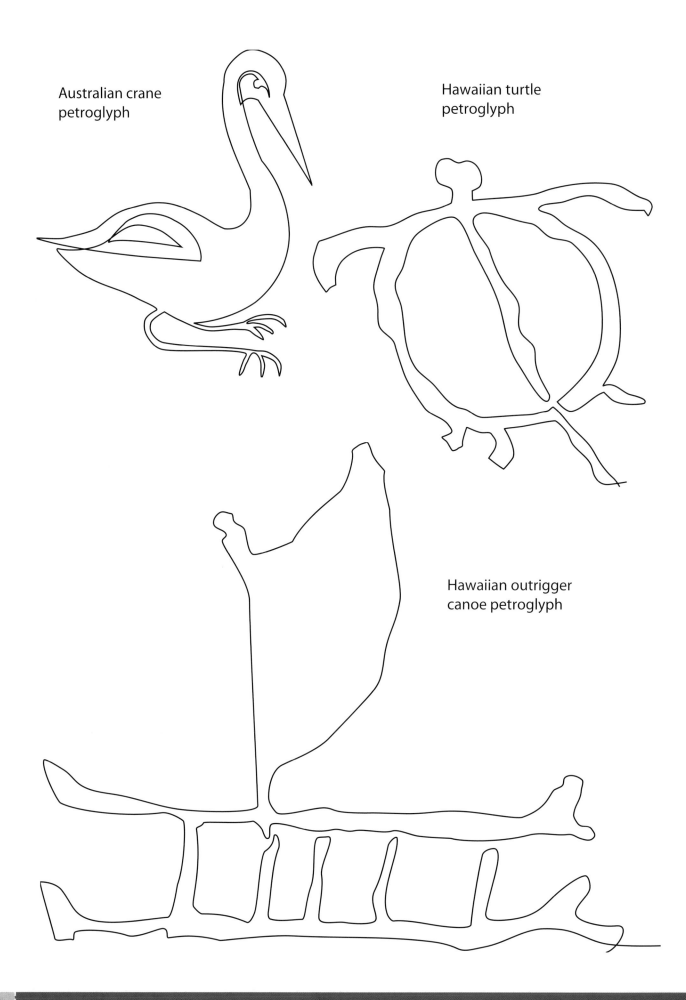

Australian crane
petroglyph

Hawaiian turtle
petroglyph

Hawaiian outrigger
canoe petroglyph

Aboriginal petroglyphs

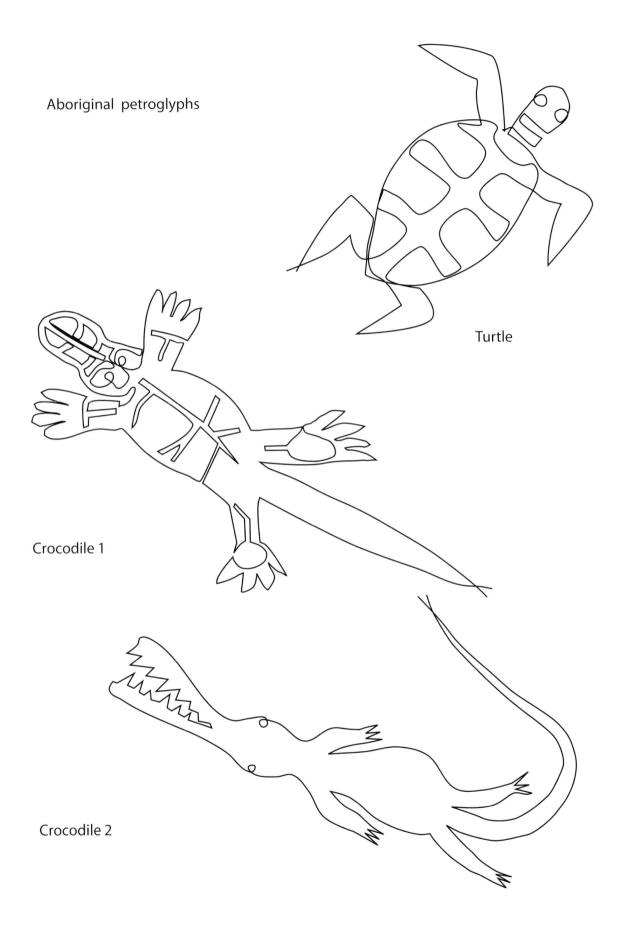

Turtle

Crocodile 1

Crocodile 2

Australian petroglyphs

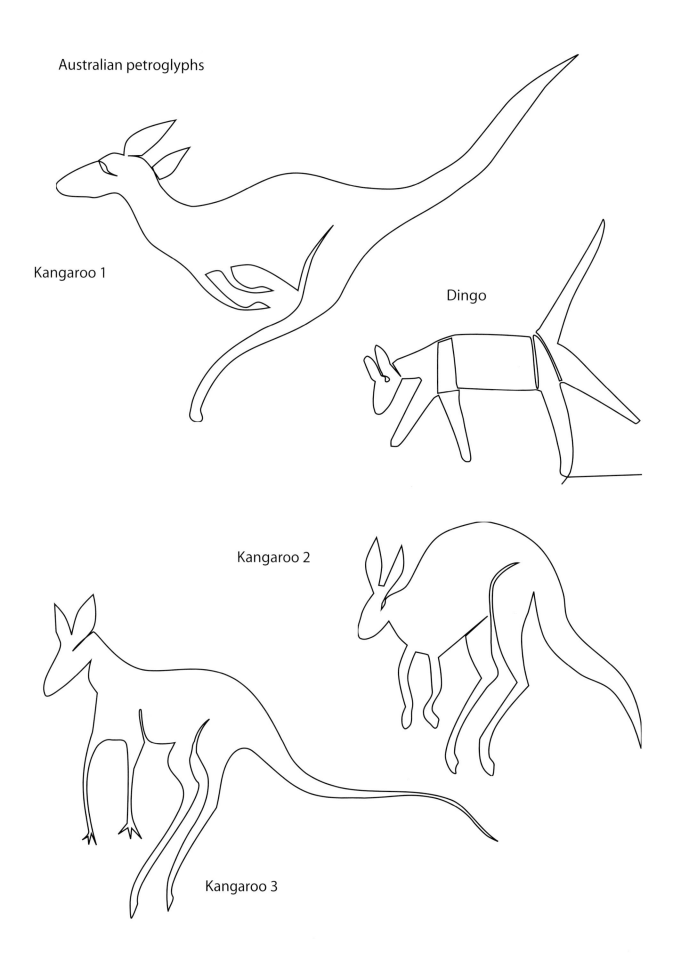

Kangaroo 1

Dingo

Kangaroo 2

Kangaroo 3

Australian animals

Kiwi bird

Koala and baby

Koala in gum tree

Chinese Junk

Chinese
Lion Dancer

Mount Fuji

Mount Fuji with Cranes in flight
try quilting this 9″ tall × 20″ wide

Mount Fuji with Swans

Old Time Cowboys

Hollywood's cowboy movies of the early years were full of campy concepts.

Here are some "old time cowboys" images to have some fun with in the same spirit.

Hoppin' mad bucking mule

Simple little chuckwagon

Put three mules together for a bucking border

Longhorn steer

Burro

Burro in the Desert Block

Starring: Burro, co-starring: Ten gallon hat, shot on location in The High Desert.

This longhorn steer is quilted in two steps. First quilt the Monument Valley landscape to your left, then enter the longhorn's front hoof. As soon as you quilt the bottomline of his body, then the topline and face, you will exit through the tip of his horn, quilt the clouds and more landscape, then return through the same horn-tip to finish the steer, finish the landscape.

I split images this way by freehand too, it just happens.

Fancy cowboy boot

Fancy lariat work

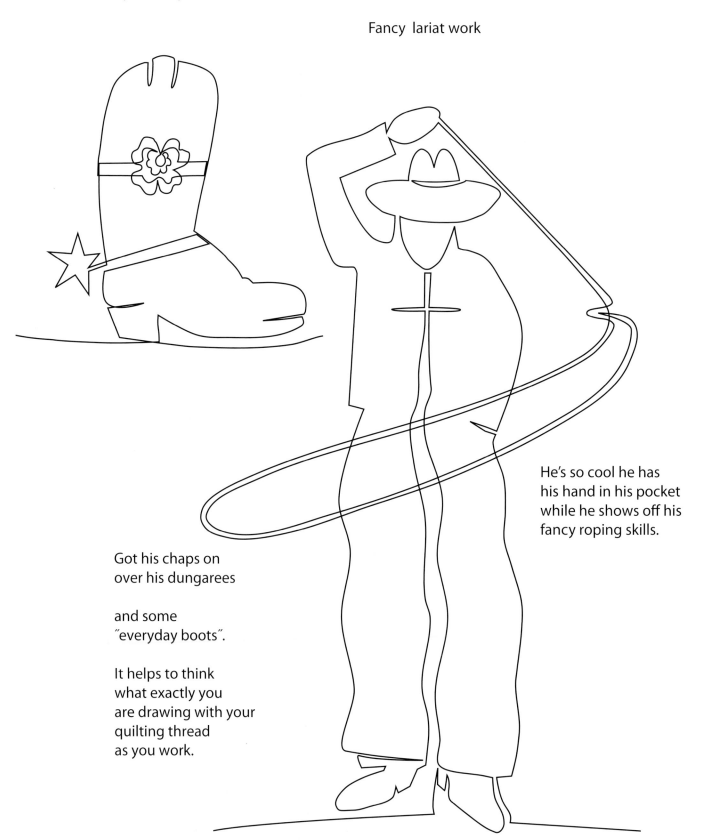

He's so cool he has
his hand in his pocket
while he shows off his
fancy roping skills.

Got his chaps on
over his dungarees

and some
"everyday boots".

It helps to think
what exactly you
are drawing with your
quilting thread
as you work.

Old time cowboy showing off at the mustang ranch Block

Perhaps cactus and craggy rocks aren't for you,

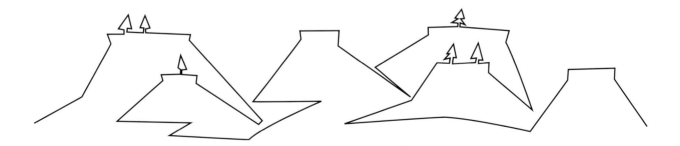

Mesa Landscape could be the right alternative.

Try substituting parts of the mesa landscape
into the cowboy and mustang block above.

Tortoise and the Lariat Block

Painted Desert

Two Southwest goat petroglyphs

Southwest petroglyph with prickly pear and saguaro

Canyon de
Chelly pictograph

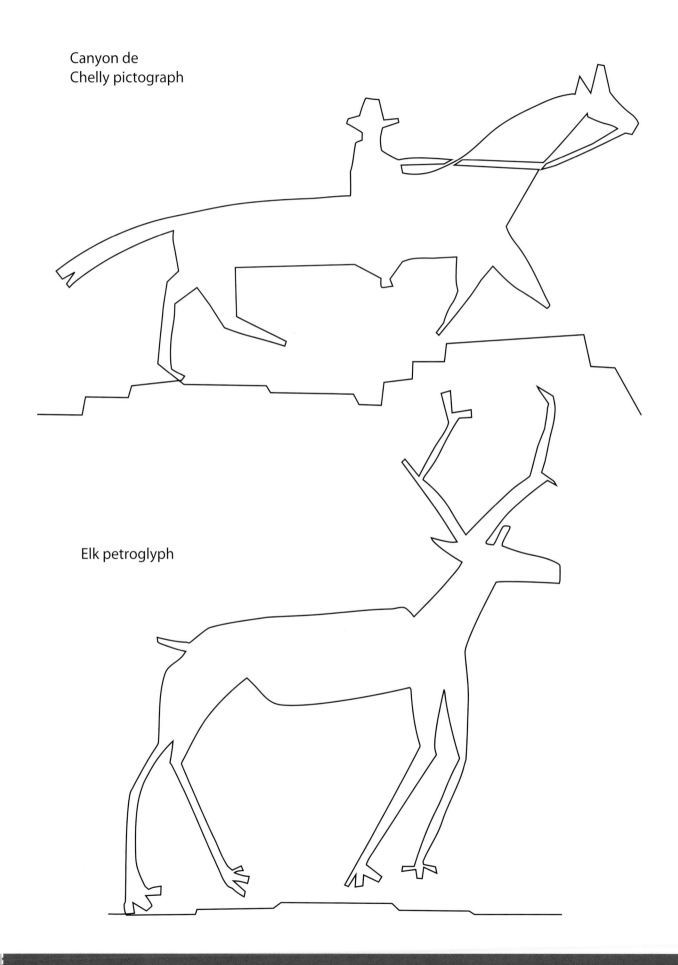

Elk petroglyph

American Southwest

Petroglyphs

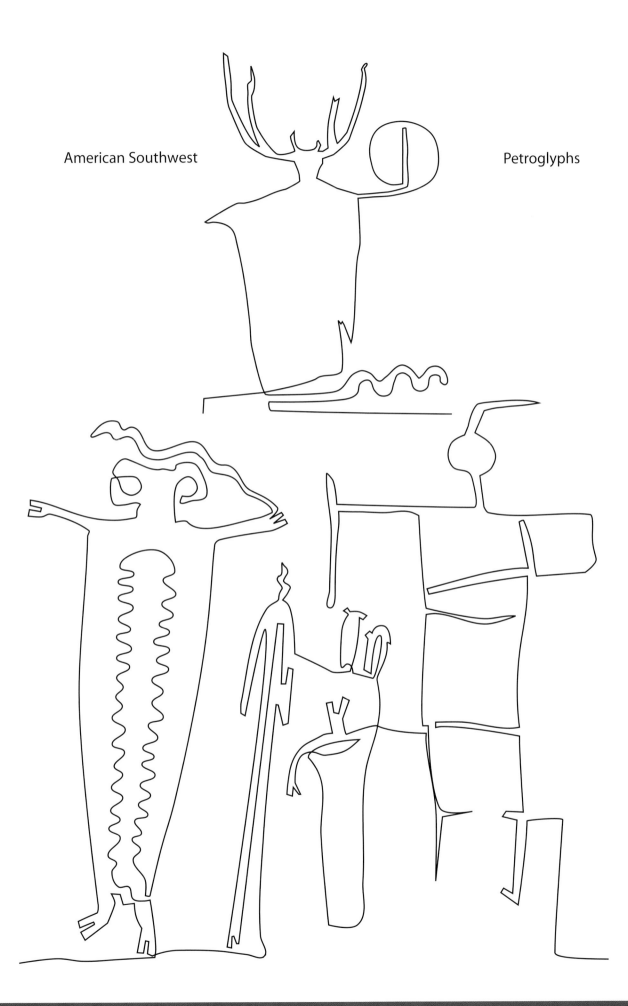

Got an Angle?
SCROLLS AND ANGLES

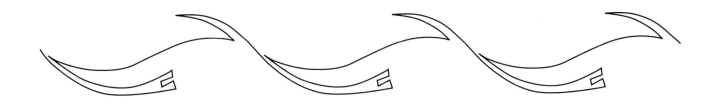

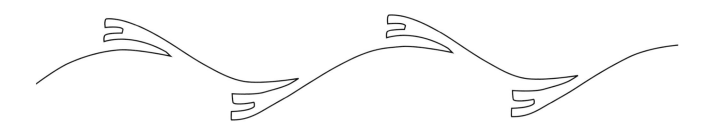

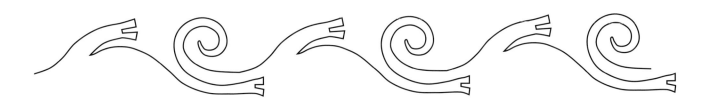

Scroll Theme and variations

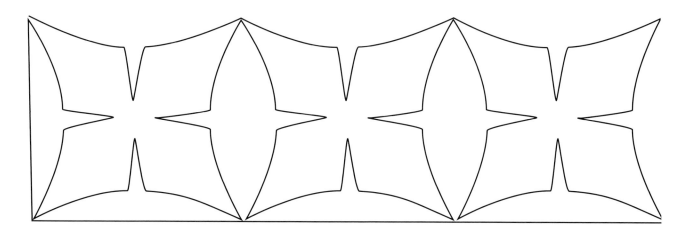

Laura's secret border

See it quilted at the beginning of this section, in a three-row block.

Reindeer scroll border

Big dogs scroll border

Flying dog scroll border

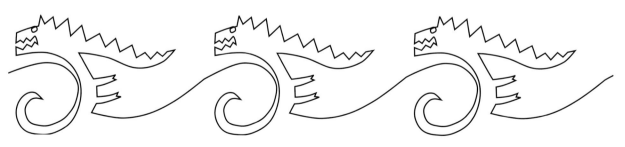

Dragon scroll border

'Fritz Triple' Braided border

First border alone, for example this shows 4 repeats ,"cap" at start (at left), no turning corners

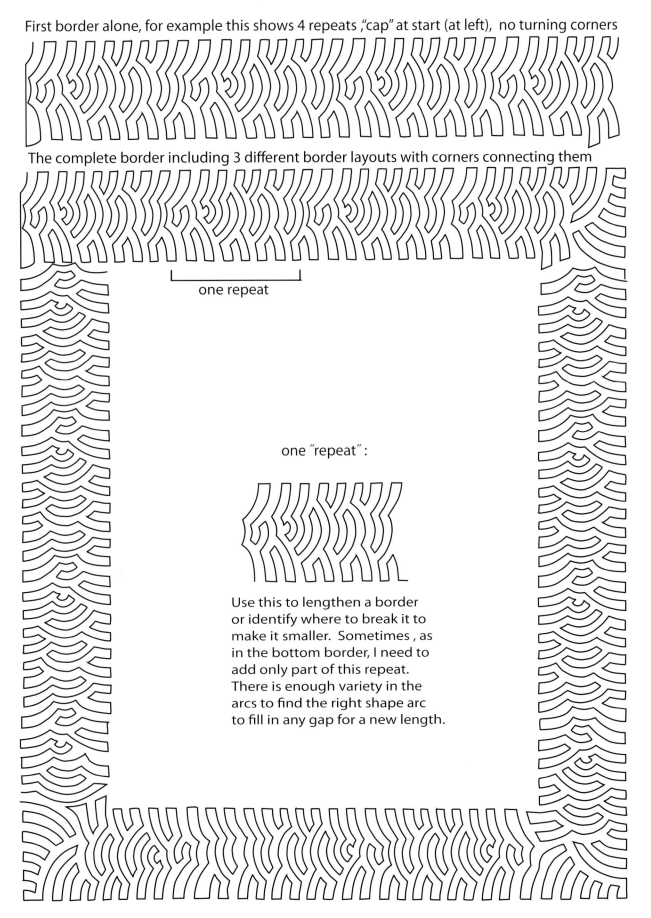

The complete border including 3 different border layouts with corners connecting them

one repeat

one "repeat" :

Use this to lengthen a border
or identify where to break it to
make it smaller. Sometimes , as
in the bottom border, I need to
add only part of this repeat.
There is enough variety in the
arcs to find the right shape arc
to fill in any gap for a new length.

Fritz Triple Braid , below, as a block

Left border

Right border

This is a turning corner. See how it fits into the "right border" and again on the bottom border. Look for it on the full border page, it is on three border corners.

Both the left border and the right border are worked downward from the top.

Third, or bottom, border work from right to left.

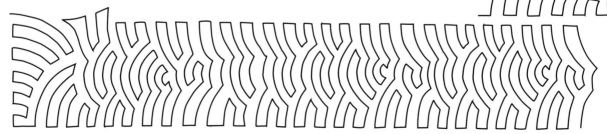

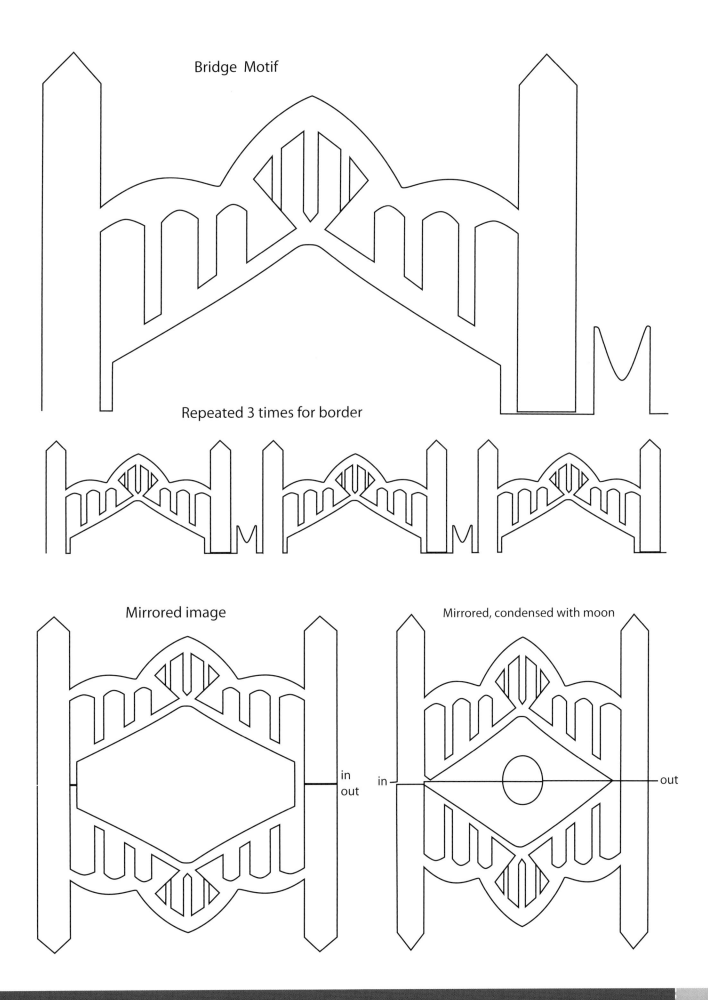

Bridge Motif

Repeated 3 times for border

Mirrored image

in
out

Mirrored, condensed with moon

in

out

Curly Key border one motif:

Curly Key border motif mirrored and repeated, with "caps" to join ends:

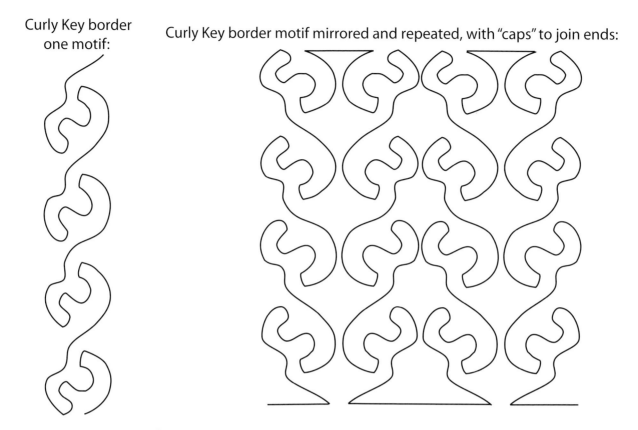

Curly key border motif staggered, repeated, with "caps" to join ends:

Knot Block Motif

Knot motif

Variation 1: as rectangular border

Variation 2: motif with petaled corners

About the Author

LAURA LEE FRITZ is widely known for her hand appliqué quilts and her fanciful wholecloth quilting filled with narrative images from the stories surrounding her life. Laura raises bluetick hounds and Navajo-Icelandic sheep in rural Marin County, California, but slips off of the farm to teach quilting classes from Napa Valley College in California to her long-arm machine quilting classes at the annual International Quilt Festival in Houston.

Laura Lee Fritz

31 Glen Road

Novato, CA 94945

415-320-4369

www.lauraleefritz.com

Resources

Batting

Hobbs Bonded Fibers

200 South Commerce Dr.

Waco, TX 76702

800-433-3357

www.hobbsbondedfibers.com/quilters.html

Matilda's Own

JT Trading Corporation

1200 Main Street

Bridgeport, CT 06601

203-339-4904

Quilter's Dream

589 Central Drive

Virginia Beach, VA 23454

888-268-8664

www.quiltersdreambatting.com

The Warm Company

5529 186th Place SW

Lynnwood, WA 98037

425-248-2424

www.warmcompany.com

Threads

American & Efird, Inc.

400 East Central Ave.

Mount Holly, NC 28120

800-438-0545

www.amefird.com

Superior Threads

87 East 2580 South

St. George, UT 84790

800-499-1777

www.superiorthreads.com

YLI Corporation

1439 Dave Lyle Blvd. #16C

Rock Hill, SC 29730

803-985-3100

www.ylicorp.com

Water-Soluble Stabilizer

Solvy Wash-Away Stabilizer

Sulky of America

980 Cobb Place Blvd., Suite 130

Kennesaw, GA 30144

800-874-4115

www.sulky.com

Dissolve Stabilizer

Superior Threads

87 East 2580 South

St. George, UT 84790

800-499-1777

www.superiorthreads.com

More Books by Laura Lee Fritz

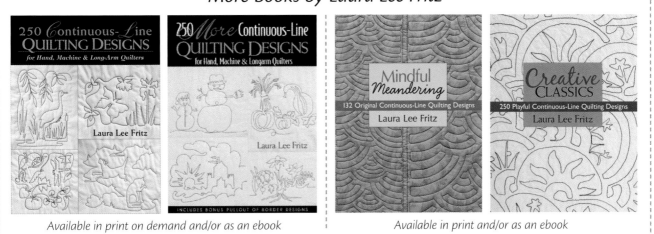

Available in print on demand and/or as an ebook   *Available in print and/or as an ebook*

Great Titles *from* C&T PUBLISHING

Available at your local retailer or **www.ctpub.com** *or* **800-284-1114**

*For a list of other fine books from C&T Publishing, visit our website
to view our catalog online.*

C&T PUBLISHING, INC.

P.O. Box 1456
Lafayette, CA 94549
800-284-1114

Email: ctinfo@ctpub.com
Website: www.ctpub.com

*C&T Publishing's professional photography services are now available to
the public. Visit us at www.ctmediaservices.com.*

Tips and Techniques *can be found at www.ctpub.com > Consumer
Resources > Quiltmaking Basics: Tips & Techniques for Quiltmaking & More*

For quilting supplies:

COTTON PATCH

1025 Brown Ave.
Lafayette, CA 94549
Store: 925-284-1177
Mail order: 925-283-7883

Email: CottonPa@aol.com
Website: www.quiltusa.com

*Note: Fabrics used in the quilts shown may not be currently
available, as fabric manufacturers keep most fabrics in print for
only a short time.*